A World of Colors

Un Mundo de Colores

by Honey & Poppy

Copyright © 2025 Honey & Poppy's World
(Cynthia Monroe & Matthew Monroe)
All rights reserved.

No part of this publication may be reproduced, stored in a retrieval system, or transmitted in any form or by any means — electronic, mechanical, photocopying, recording, or otherwise without the prior written permission of the publisher, except in the case of brief quotations used in reviews or educational settings.

ISBN (Paperback): 979-8-9930905-2-8
ISBN (Hardcover): 979-8-9930905-6-6
Library of Congress Control Number (Paperback): 2025920797
Library of Congress Control Number (Hardcover): 2025925783

Published by Honey & Poppy's World
honeyandpoppysworld.com

Printed in the United States of America
Illustrations created and designed by Honey.

Welcome, little color explorer...

The world is brighter with you in it.
May you always see beauty in every color.

• • •

Bienvenido, pequeño explorador de colores...

El mundo es más brillante contigo en él.
Que siempre veas la belleza en cada color.

Red
rojo

little red wagon
carrito rojo

red truck
camión rojo

Red
rojo

red chile
chile rojo

red heart
corazón rojo

red bus
autobús rojo

Amarillo
yellow

pato amarillo
yellow duck

elote (maíz) amarillo
yellow corn

Amarillo
yellow

lápiz amarillo
yellow pencil

sol amarillo
yellow sun

Blue
azul

blue shirt

camisa azul

blue balloons

globos azules

Blue
azul

blue shoes
zapatos azules

blue bird
pájaro azul

Verde
green

rana verde
green frog

manzana verde
green apple

Verde
green

palmera verde
green palm tree

chile verde
green chile

Orange
naranja

orange cat
gato naranja

orange clownfish
pez payaso naranja

Orange
naranja

orange pumpkin
calabaza naranja

orange (fruit)
naranja (fruta) naranja

Morado
purple

mariposa morada
purple butterfly

crayón morado
purple crayon

Morado
purple

flores moradas
purple flowers

uvas moradas
purple grapes

Pink
rosa

pink ice cream
helado rosa

pink teddy bear
oso de peluche rosa

Pink
rosa

pink flamingo
flamenco rosa

pink piglet
cerdito rosa

Café (Marrón)
brown

guitarra café
brown guitar

perro café
brown dog

Café (Marrón)
brown

camello café
brown camel

tambor café
brown drum

Black
negro

black horse
caballo negro

black dog
perro negro

Black
negro

black hat
sombrero negro

black spider
araña negra

Blanco
white

nieve blanca
white snow

leche blanca
white milk

Blanco
white

conejito blanco
white bunny

oso polar blanco
white polar bear

Gray
gris

gray elephant
elefante gris

gray mouse
ratón gris

Gray
gris

gray koala
koala gris

gray donkey
burro gris

Oro
gold

saxofón de oro
gold saxophone

corona de oro
gold crown

Oro
gold

tesoro de oro
gold treasure

campana de oro
gold bell

Silver
plata

silver star
estrella de plata

silver key
llave de plata

Silver
plata

silver robot
robot de plata

silver spoon
cuchara de plata

En Blanco y Negro
black and white

pingüinos de blanco y negro
black and white penguins

teclas de piano en blanco y negro
black and white piano keys

En Blanco y Negro
black and white

cebra de blanco y negro
black and white zebra

panda de blanco y negro
black and white panda

Many Colors
muchos colores

papalotes de muchos colores
kites of many colors

piñata de muchos colores
piñata of many colors

Many Colors
muchos colores

máscara de muchos colores
mask of many colors

muñecas Rusas de muchos colores
Russian dolls of many colors

Many colors, one beautiful world.

Muchos colores, un mundo hermoso.

🎵 Colors Songs

Sing along with Honey & Poppy's
A World of Colors song and other learning songs!
Scan the blue QR code below.

🗣️ Spanish Pronunciation Guides

Scan below to learn how to pronounce colors, numbers, and letters in Spanish.

About the Authors

Honey & Poppy are the heart and soul behind Honey & Poppy's World, a creative world of storytelling, learning, music, and imagination inspired by tradition and their real-life adventures.

They lovingly create early learning and educational content that introduces children to foundational ideas with a broader view of the world. Some titles are bilingual and multilingual, reflecting a belief that people, differences, and children everywhere matter, and that early exposure helps build confident, curious, open-hearted learners.

Their work celebrates decades of parenting, travel, big family moments, and everyday magic, designed to connect generations.

Other Titles from Honey & Poppy's World

<u>Available Now</u>
A World of Colors – Un Mundo de Colores
A World of Colors – Un Mundo de Colores: Companion Coloring Book
A World of Numbers – Un Mundo de Números
Mixing Colors with Zach & Kona
Mixing Colors with Zach & Kona: Companion Coloring Book
Meet Zach & Kona: The Desert Dogs
Honey Has the Flu: Flu Fighters on Duty
Hushabye and Goodnight

<u>Coming Soon!</u>
A World of Letters – Un Mundo de Letras
A World of Words – Un Mundo de Palabras
Exploring Our World: Antarctica
A World of Fluffy Friends: Wildlife of the Rocky Mountains

For the curious children
in every corner of the world...

We'll be here when you are
ready for more: ABCs, 123s,
A World of Fluffy Friends,
and many more Wonders of the World.

• • •

Para los niños curiosos
en cada rincón del mundo...

Aquí estaremos cuando estés
listo para más: ABCs, 123s,
Un Mundo de Amigos Suavecitos,
y muchas más Maravillas del Mundo.